BEFORE YOU START

Jeanna Booker

Copyright © 2025 by Jeanna Booker
All rights reserved.

No part of this book may be reproduced, stored in a retrieval system, or transmitted in any form or by any means, electronic, mechanical, photocopying, recording, or otherwise, without the prior written permission of the author, except for the use of brief quotations in a book review or scholarly journal.

ISBN: 979-8-9990149-2-4
Cover Design by: Jeanna B. Creative

For information about permissions, contact:
Jeanna Booker
JeannaBCreative@gmail.com
JeannaBCreative.com

DEDICATION

I write this book with a heart overflowing with gratitude for the beloved Kimberly Smith, affectionately known as Mama Kim. Though she has passed on to Glory, the seeds she sowed and the legacy she left behind continues to live on. Thank you, Mama Kim, for pouring into me and the entire Pearl Empire with unwavering love and wisdom.

To 13:46 Dance Ensemble, The Pearl Empire, you have been instrumental in equipping me with hands-on training in learning to build with Holy Spirit. For loving me, pushing me, and holding my ladder as I am cultivated into the Pearl of Great Price that God has called me to be, I am forever thankful.

To Apostle Raine, thank you for being a voice in the earth that has declared God's word over my life. Let June 30, 2023, be marked as "The Line of Distinction", the moment when the authority in my voice was restored. Thank you for being the vessel through which God's word was spoken, "If you open your mouth, I'll fill it."

Lastly, to my leader, Apostle Yolanda Stith, thank you for your prayers, wisdom, love, declarations, guidance, leadership by example, and unwavering covering. I am truly grateful.

With deep gratitude and love, thank you.

CONTENT

Introduction……………………………………………………..1

1. The Why………………………………………………….3

2. The Mission……………………………………………...7

3. The Difference…………………………………………..11

4. The Name………………………………………………..15

5. The Launch……………………………………………...19

6. The Brand……………………………………………….23

7. The Audience……………………………………………27

8. The Comparison………………………………………...29

9. The Mind………………………………………………..33

10. The Problem……………………………………………37

11. The Solution……………………………………………41

12. The Prayer……………………………………………...45

Live Your Dreams Challenge………………………………….49

INTRODUCTION

The room is all white, stale, and empty. It's chilly and your skin is forming goosebumps from the breeze coming from the open window. While sitting in the middle of the floor, there is a blank sheet of paper, and in your right hand, a brand new ink pen. You're eager, excited, and ready to write down all the details of your next creation, but you're stuck, lost with a lack of inspiration. The longer you try to find where to start, the more anxious you become. As you reach your breaking point, immediately there's a warm breath of wind drawing your attention to the open window. Hesitantly, you stand up, walk towards the window, and glance out of it as you approach. A few steps on the other side of the window is a wooden ladder. Full of curiosity, you climb through the window. As you gather yourself on the other side, you take in an amazing sight. You see a beautiful land full of colors and hues you've never experienced before. You reach for the ladder. The moment your skin touches it, you feel an inviting connection welcoming you to climb. With each step up the ladder, the colorful

Introduction

scenery becomes further and further away. You begin to pass fluffy white clouds as you continue to ascend the ladder. The air becomes crystal clear and wonderful to breathe in and out. As you reach the top of the ladder, you enter Heaven. As you explore your surroundings, you come across an overwhelming angelic sight - bright, warm, and leaves you speechless. You are encountering the throne of God. Directly in front of the throne is an extremely long grand table. As a formal family style dinner, the table is set with hundreds of bowls and dishes. Like a child being called to dinner, you cheerfully run over to the table. Looking over the buffet on the table, you realize the dishes are full of something you were longing for. All the things you lacked back in the stale white room were now spread out along the entire table. Inspirations for ideas, guidance for creative direction, colors, titles, movements, demonstrations, resources, and so much more were overflowing from the dishes and bowls. Sitting next to the throne, at the top of the table, were glass mason jars. Thankfully and humbly you approach the throne. You collect as many mason jars as your arms can carry. Full of gratitude, you fill the jars to capacity with as much as you can from this spread of creativity. As you prepare for your climb back down the ladder, you thank the Creator as He sits on his throne. Making your way back down the ladder, towards the land full of amazing colors, you climb back through the window. You sit back in the middle of the white room. Now, after having an experience with the Master of Creation, you are able to use the pen that was in your right hand and the blank paper that was in your left hand. With your ideas flourishing, you begin to place pen to paper, releasing what Abba has placed in you. Full of purpose and intention, you are now free to create and build.

THE WHY

Let's jump right in and get this out of the way first. Financial gain should never be the inspiration or spark for starting your business. There is absolutely no longevity in a foundation based on money. The successful lifespan of a business is built with the purpose of being a solution and aligned with God's will. A business built on the principle of being solution-based will present opportunities for wealth, sustainability, and impact. When your mind starts to imagine yourself as the CEO, stop and ask yourself, "Why?". Your "why" should constantly point back to the solutions God has placed in you. Use the following as a guide to develop an intentional approach to answering 'the why' in your building journey. The most important part of this overall process is to keep God and His will for your life first. Not only should your prayer be "let your will be done", but also "align my will with your will." Your desires for business should mirror and simply be what God's desires are concerning you. As vessels in this earth, everything should reflect our heavenly father. Our lifestyles all the way down to the

The Why

businesses we lead should be the yielded results of 1) seeking him, 2) coming into agreement with his will, and 3) being obedient to what he has released you to do.

Everything falls into place when you pursue Him. Your main focus and priority should be worshipping Him, even with the existence of your business.

"But seek first the kingdom of God and His righteousness, and all these things shall be added to you." Matthew 6:33 NKJV

Seeking God, first, gives you the necessary road map and blueprints to initiate your business. As the master of creation, He has ultimate insight on creating. Prioritizing what he shows you will help everything flow and give you the ability to gracefully build. Pursuing God's desires for your business is like having access to unlimited sponsors. The evidence and fruit of you seeking first comes in the form of grace and favor.

Your "why?" should also be led by what inspires you. Steady inspiration fuels a passion behind your work, making it more likely that you will go above and beyond to keep your business alive. When personal connection is lacking, the desire and excitement to build will fade. Motivation is essential in overcoming the challenges that any business will encounter. Does your "why?" connect to your story or the challenges you have overcome in your life? God does all things well and on purpose. Don't overlook the adversity you have gone through. I like to consider the hard knocks of life Cultivation Seasons. These are times when solutions are birthed. Your process holds value and has the ability to create unique solutions for those who weren't graced to conquer the same way you have.

The Why

If there is no personal connection to your business, it will not be stable. Business is more than achieving a particular dollar amount; it's about perpetuating its growth, receiving its benefits and pouring again. You have to uncover why you choose to do what you do and what you enjoy about it.

Evaluating your passions and defining your purpose is an important factor to consider in advance. Our passion is typically what we tend to follow, but there's one small issue with that. Passion is connected to our emotions. Since our emotions are not consistent, it is not beneficial to base our goals or careers on passion alone. Purpose should be the driving force and motivation. We were all created for a reason. The hard part is identifying that reason. Passion tends to be self gratifying while purpose serves the needs of others. Take the time for introspection and determine your passion and purpose. Compare and contrast the two to determine how your purpose connects with your why and how it aligns with God's will.

When building upon God's will for you, it takes the pressure off of you. Following God's plans is like having insurance; if things go wrong or challenges arise, it gives the security to maneuver through it. He's either building your character, teaching you lessons, and/or redirecting you back on his path for your life. Either way it gives Him glory. God does not lie! If He said it, if He called you to build it, if He spoke to you concerning it, then He will back his investment. God wants you to succeed, so he'll send everything you will need to bring it to fruition. Obedience to His instructions is another way to glorify and lift his name. If there is no fruit, then what you create may be self-induced. Fruit doesn't necessarily manifest instantly, but a clear path towards it will be evident.

Your story is the gateway to your purpose. The situations we face in

The Why

life - full of pain, challenges, and even joy - mold us and build wisdom. These moments are often God's way of capturing our attention and guiding us toward the calling He's placed on our lives. Some might even call it "on-the-job training." Real-life stories of triumph consistently lay the foundation for powerful, successful brands because they are rooted in experience and resilience. They form genuine emotional connections with others, allowing your personal values and character to shine through. Through your story, God's work is amplified and makes your journey most relatable. When you share your testimony, you highlight God's undeniable power and give Him the glory. People are drawn to authenticity, not surface-level trends or profit-driven motives. They connect with the depth of your why. And it's in that "why" where you'll find alignment with your God-given purpose.

THE MISSION

The core definition of the word mission is "an important assignment carried out". The same way the Lord calls us to different things throughout life, is the same way he assigns us to launch and pursue the birth of different businesses and organizations. The success of what you build is connected to how committed you are to living out the mission assigned to what is created. A mission statement defines the company's business, its objectives, and its approach to reach those objectives. It provides a clearly stated purpose of your business and the goals. A mission statement also clarifies the function and intention of an organization. It should identify your primary audience and the type of products or services you produce.

Create your mission statement after seeking God for clarity and insight. It is imperative that you hear his voice and not your own during this process. You are literally building the road map to what's to come from what you are building. Embrace it; however, be open

The Mission

to change if there's a prompt from Holy Spirit. Your mission statement will help you make decisions as you grow. Make sure as you expand and evolve, the substance of your brand should reflect your mission statement. The focus should be offering services or products consistent with your brand, not competing with trends on social platforms. Trending with what's popular may offer quick short term reward, but could cause long term damage by providing a false perception of your brand's authenticity. The mission statement should aid towards long term success and stability, rather than quick gains.

Revisiting the mission statement during what may seem like a slow or hard season will reignite your initial thoughts and reconnect you with your purpose in business. If the mission is based upon God's will, it will always be a great source of a quick guide. You should be able to ask yourself, "Does this service connect to my mission?". If it doesn't, just save it for another season after God has led you to write out a new statement or launch a new brand. You may be called to birth one brand or several. There is no limit to what God can do. That's why it's important to continue to seek him for guidance and make sure you are in agreement with his will. Being out of alignment and creating your own mission here on this earth could cause some unnecessary hardships. One way to be a partaker of the rewards of obedience is by staying committed to the mission.

Having a brand with a clear mission derives from a strong foundation and aids in connecting to your audience. It builds trust with customers to help them understand your purpose beyond selling them a product or service. It gives authenticity to the solution you are offering. When your audience sees consistency between your actions and mission, it fosters loyalty and trust.

Having a well organized mission will help create a strong loyal team.

The Mission

When your team understands the brand's purpose, it gives them the opportunity to fully engage, align, and commit to the vision. Everyone will be able to get on the same page and build while speaking the same language and conveying the overall goal. A clear mission not only fortifies how a brand presents itself but also influences every aspect of its operations.

THE DIFFERENCE

During varied stages of building, you may find that what you are creating looks similar to, or in the same industry as those around you. No worries! Embrace it as motivation to help you settle in reflection to redefine what makes you unique. A great example is the church. There are so many different church options, everywhere, with in-person and virtual options. However, there is something specific (or unique) that draws you to one church over another. Maybe it's the amazing worship experience during praise and worship, the preached word, the greeter's smiling face, or something as simple as the cleanliness of the bathroom. Or, the audio quality one ministry may prioritize in their online experience compared to the warm welcome of another ministry's in-person encounter. One church's uniqueness will often differ from the next ministry, and that is what sets every church apart.

The difference of attraction (of your business), can be identified by your individual strengths and weaknesses. If you are creating a

The Difference

dance company with years of ballet training, the obvious foundation of all your student training should be ballet, as opposed to hip hop dance. You will excel when you are aware of what makes your brand strong. Awareness of your foundation and target audience will create an effective experience for those consumers. Knowing "what makes you unique" (your why and inspiration) will be the fuel that keeps you set apart.

Creating in the comfort of your own uniqueness will allow you to birth services that cannot be copied - even when others try. Unfortunately, there are some people who find no fault in building without seeking by using the foundation and ideas of what others have worked hard to birth, for their own success. However, the passion, inspiration, and anointing that form the manifestation of your creations cannot be duplicated.

Exemplifying the difference in your mission statement will also be beneficial to help your brand stand out. While many brands offer similar products or services, a brand with a distinct mission can create its own niche or lane. Customers who connect to the brand's values will be drawn to its authenticity, even with a similarity to other brands. Additionally, exceptional customer service and memorable experiences will amplify personalized interactions, maintaining customer retention and satisfaction - making the experience you offer one of a kind. Successful businesses are determined by excellence in problem solving. Your solution-based approach will illuminate the uniqueness of your brand. One's uniqueness is established by their individual life experiences: the educational background, upbringing, and hardships we have endured and overcome all build character which make us stronger individuals. When we create businesses, the same life skills we have adopted are able to be used as leverage. As a result, we are left with

The Difference

personalized traits that only our business can offer. Though others may share similar backstories, your story is unique for the business birthed within you. You are the difference! Authenticity and relatability help build trust and emotional connection with customers, all while highlighting what makes you separate from everyone else.

Keeping your business distinct in a competitive market is crucial for growth and success. You can attain this by providing or creating that which your audience can identify. Develop a plan that sets your business apart. It could be your reception to customer feedback or feedback or effective product delivery. For example, if you were a nail tech, others in the industry may focus on nail design curating a luxury experience in a nail studio with a high end feel, while your intention and focus is nail care. Therefore, your client's service could be aimed to have beautiful nails from the inside out, not just a design placed on top; nail care versus nail design. When promoting, your marketing tool would gain the attention of those who desire long lasting healthy nails. Being conscious of creating a tailored solution will formulate your intended client community.

Your community should feel distinctly different from others. Whether that difference comes from your personality, your product, the customer experience, or even the way people interact with your brand, the key is to create a space where customers feel a sense of peace and belonging. A community doesn't just happen - it forms intentionally when you build something people can trust. When customers know your brand is dependable and consistent, they'll naturally begin to invest their time, energy, and loyalty. People naturally compare products, but once someone experiences your brand and recognizes its quality, they become immersed in the community that surrounds it. That unique sense of connection should make them want to stay and not search elsewhere. By

The Difference

intentionally crafting this environment, your business can stand out and foster a loyal customer base that values your authenticity and difference.

THE NAME

The foundation of the identity of what you are building must be secured from the start. The name you decide to label who you are and where you plan on going will either set you up for a path of success and growth or a shaky, unstable journey that highlights and promotes confusion and doubt.

One of my favorite things to keep in mind is does the name encourage dialog. It should be catchy enough to make someone say "hmmm" when they hear it but still not cliche. Having a name that can spark someone's interest gives the opportunity to expand your reach beyond your immediate circle. Those conversational opportunities that are created from the name should be used to share your why and connect. If done properly, you should be able to gain a wider audience.

For those that are establishing Christian brands, please be certain of where and who God has called you to. If your goal is to reach the

The Name

unsaved, having a churchy name that screams this is a christian brand shouldn't be the first choice. The name should embody Christ's light but not necessarily with words. You want to introduce them to his principles while building relationships. Some people have preset ideas of christianian and won't even give it a chance. Having a unique name for your brand whose core represents God's kingdom, will give more opportunity to rooms and platforms. Your brand may be the closest they get to the church, you don't have to beat it over there head. For example, let's create a christian airline. Our goal is to offer affordable flights that still feel luxurious. A churchy name would be, Up Hither Airways and the tag line would be "fly for the low so you can seek up high". Now that is churchy. A more relatable and approachable name could be, Halom Airways and tag line would be "a flight that gives clarity". Halom is the Hebrew word for hither. The tagline will instantly speak to the spirit of all who encounter it. Branding could push the luxury yet relaxing experience that will prompt reflection and clear thoughts.

Another effective approach to choosing a business name that connects with your brand identity is to consider the response you want to evoke. Ask yourself: What feeling do you want people to experience when they hear your business name? How do you want consumers to think, react, or perceive your business? What key question do you want to come to mind when hearing your business name?". You want to always leave an opportunity to network and display your brand. Those questions will assist in reaching that goal. The name should be able to be a conversation starter.

Another key point to explore is the availability of the name. Make sure to do your research and check if the name is already in use. Look up your state's business registry to confirm it hasn't been claimed by someone else. Before you finalize your decision, ensure

The Name

the name isn't already trademarked or associated with another brand. Also, check for available domain names and social media handles. You want to make sure you give yourself the ability to be consistent across all platforms.

While researching that, simply google it. You should be aware of what else people will come across when they are trying to find information on your brand. Depending on what comes up, you may need to adjust your name to protect your brand from being connected to random negative or non beneficial searches. Everyone wont always read all details that may come up when searching. It would be a shame to lose potential clients because of a mistake in brand identity or from what comes up surrounding your business.

The name you choose should have staying power. You don't want it to feel outdated after your first trip around the sun. Keep in mind how the name might age as your brand evolves or if it will still fit as your brand expands. That's another reason why it's important to seek God during the early stages and throughout building. As the ultimate creator, He's guaranteed to release a timeless name to you.

If God has called you to be an international brand, be sure the name does not offend the culture of your audience beyond borders. The name should be safe to use in all cultures and not have any negative or inappropriate meanings or translations.

THE LAUNCH

I know you are excited and you just received the raw, unedited pics from your photoshoot you recently completed, but this shouldn't be the first thing people see when you officially launch! Respectfully, take a step back!) When we've envisioned something for any amount of time and finally have the opportunity to release it in the earth, we tend to get overzealous and start releasing our brands before it's even able to hold its head up on its own, like a baby. We have one time to make a great, lasting first impression; make it count.

When preparing for your launch, be sure to cross your T's and dot your I's. You should present your brand in excellence. However, please do not confuse this with perfection. The Bible encourages us not to despise small beginnings. Though you may be just starting out and starting with a small budget, this doesn't give you the green light to just release any ol thing. The beauty of starting from scratch is it forces you to rely on God more and seek him for more creative ways to make something out of nothing. You may not have

The Launch

a few hundred dollars to cover a billboard with your logo, but you do have the ability to give your well prepared 30 second elevator speech at each opportunity that presents itself for absolutely no cost. Moving with Holy Spirit and having God's favor will get your brand further than any budget available. From the moment you launch, be sure God is in every step of the process.

Launching in God's timing will determine how gracefully you are able to handle challenges when they arise. There will always be all kinds of mishaps and unplanned hiccups, but when in God's time and will, you will be fully prepared to overcome those situations without it being a burden. Favor will flow and direct you to the best way to get past it. If your building journey is full of constant setbacks or hardships that seem impossible to get through, you most likely have misfired your launching time. Jumping ahead of God's time is a self setup for delayed reward. God very much could have given you a full vision, with ideas, never before heard of creations, and even the perfect name to call your brand. Unfortunately, if you don't go back to God and ask him when to release all the amazing things he has shown you, it could be out of season, which brings on unnecessary hindrances. Save yourself some time, energy, and find peace by simply waiting for God to give you the ordained time.

Preparation for launching should also include market research. Having a practical understanding of the industry you are launching into will encourage a path of success. Being aware of the demand for your product or service is necessary to partner with your instructions from Holy Spirit. Being connected to Holy Spirit will guide you to time your release when demand is high or when the need for it is relevant. This may seem a little silly, but releasing a new snow boot line in the middle of May would be considered poor timing. Do the work to understand seasonal trends and trends of

The Launch

the consumers of your product. Attention to details like this will set you up for a successful launch.

Leading up to the launch you should also be building anticipation, but without giving too many details. By creating a buzz before the official launch, you are already planting seeds to grow into a community for your brand. You can catch their interest by using teasers, social media posts, and sneak peeks behind the scenes. The key is to only show just enough to capture their attention and wanting more without prematurely introducing the product.

Some other factors to consider before your launch include being aware of when others in the same industry are releasing new services or products, ensuring your products are fully developed and tested, and making sure you are mentally, physically, spiritually, and emotionally prepared to start this journey. This will give you an advantage and prevent rushed releases that could damage your brand's reputation. Timing it when everything is in place will lead to your customers or audience having a positive experience. Set your business up on a smooth path by ensuring you're fully prepared in all areas.

THE BRAND

Creating, understanding, knowing, communicating and identifying your brand is necessary before your public release. Of course, some things are developed over time; however, if you have the opportunity to have things in place, you will be able to build more efficiently. Your logo, style, look, colors of your brand should be intentionally developed. It should reflect the mission, values, and purpose of your business that connects to your audience. For example, the colors used on a bottle of kids shampoo could be multicolored with patterns. While a male brand shampoo could be minimalistic, bold, and monotone.

Being consistent with your brand builds trust with your clientele and makes it recognizable. From the website, the social media pages, marketing materials, packaging, and even your exchange with your audience; everything should have some type of streamline that connects it all. Your website may be upbeat and full of light, but your in person interaction is dull and unfriendly, is a flawed

The Brand

foundation. Creating the brand should be led by Holy Spirit, partnered with your story, and put in place with practicality and wisdom.

Branding is one area where there is a thin line between being resourceful and making an investment. Investing in high-quality professional images and advertisements will determine how seriously your audience will take you. Elevating your brand with amazing photos and material will help bring valued customers or clientele to your brand. Everything you produce should live up to your brand's standard. Your audience will treat it the same way you do. Professionalism across all boards will communicate the authenticity of your brand.

Some businesses require for there to be a face to the brand. In those instances, a professional headshot should always be used. Cropped pictures from a phone selfie are never appropriate. If that is all you have at the time, slow down and build at a pace that is aligned with the resources you have access to. If this is God's will, every resource or financial obligation to obtain that resource will be released to you. If you seem to be at a roadblock in your building process and unable to create in excellence, returning back to God for further direction, timing, and instructions should be your resolve.

Though you are building a foundation with your brand to have a particular look and feel, be open to flexibility when Holy Spirit gives you the nudge. With all things, change is one of the only elements that will always be guaranteed. Sometimes a pivot in direction for your brand will come as the result of growth in your own maturing, the increase of your capacity the Lord has mantled you with, another part of your story God has instructed you to share, or even your audience growing. Adaptability helps you keep

The Brand

evolving your brand in a healthy way, which not only will keep you in God's timing , but also connects you to society and their needs. Our culture and technology in today's world are ever revolving. Constant check-ins with Holy Spirit will guide you with shifting as the industry you are called to shifts.

Building a strong aligned brand postures your business to attract your target audience with lasting relationships. Your branding creates a unique experience for your clientele. It will help deepen the connection between your brand, your audience, and even you. Intentionally choosing how to show and promote your brand matters. Having witty ideas to replace shortcomings is not the same as cutting corners or moving too fast. God-sent ideas, no matter the cost, will always push your brand further than the most expensive element you may add. Asking God to direct you to who should make your logo, the colors of your brand, or how things should look to the consumer will affect the viewer's experience. The balance of following God's instructions with practical preparation is the key to not only a successful launch but also a growing brand.

THE AUDIENCE

As you grow, be sure to stay at Abbas' feet and thank Him along the way. Seeing your numbers increase and the applause of man could very easily let the spirit of Pride and Greed sneak in. Constantly submitting your brand to God will prevent you from making an idol of your audience or your brand. Your clientele, each customer, and every person in the community created from your brand ultimately belongs to God. It is our job to serve his people with the product or service he has placed in you and cultivated through your testimony. Even the story that plays out in your life is still God's; you're just the vessel He chose to use to release it in the earth.

Having a heart for your customer will help you use your brand to speak directly to their needs and desires. Taking the time and effort to understand and research them will help personalize an experience just for them. Knowing the necessary tone, language, and visuals for your community to best receive you should be a part of your branding process.

The Audience

Referring to your why will always help you evaluate and connect you to your audience. As the consumer of your product or service, they will help be the mouthpiece of your brand. Word of mouth is one of the best kinds of exposure. It promotes real life experiences of those who have come into contact with your brand and expands its reach, all while displaying the business for free. Taking their feedback back to God and asking for clarity is a great way to test if you are in alignment with the purpose God said for your business. Their experience should be the solution to the problem God directed you to solve. Even with positive feedback, if it's not in God's will for you, it becomes a distraction for what He wants for you to achieve. Good outcomes do not compare to the abundant and exceeding outcomes the Lord has for you.

Be sure not to let your audience direct the journey of your business. Their desires should always be partnered with revelation and guidance from God. Just because they ask for a particular service or product, doesn't give you the green like to produce it. Being confident in the directions God gave you will help you stay on course. Even if your audience suggests something harmless or innovative, if it's not in line with what Abba designed for you to create, you and your brand are out of position.

Though we are following the voice of God first, getting reviews can still be a part of the balance and growth process. It just should not solely guide you on its own. Collecting reviews can be used to create content to expose your brand. Publicly sharing positive critique gives those considering your brand or unsure if they should give your product a chance to see the capabilities of it. By keeping your purpose in line, knowing the heart of your audience, and understanding how your brand's identity connects to God's direction and your story, you can help ensure that the community around your brand is God sent.

THE COMPARISON

One thing for sure, before you start any business, you must be confident in who you are and the brand you are going to back. Lack of confidence in an industry that is full of hundreds of people selling the same or similar products will open the door for comparison. Comparing your brand takes your focus off of what God has designed you for and the works he has others doing in the earth.

Success doesn't happen overnight. When looking at other brands, you only see the public results of what they may have struggled with privately. In today's society, we normally have access to highlights of brands via social media. We aren't privy to what leads up to that highlight.

Focusing on your own journey and realizing that you are building on your own timeline will help remove negative comparison. You should only be inspired by the success of other brands. Do not feel discouraged when your current growth doesn't look like what you

The Comparison

see in others. Let them simply build your optimism, improve your strategy, turn you back to Abba, and use it as a learning tool. A healthy way to manage comparison is by taking note of your own progression, but use it to just highlight how the Lord has expanded you.

Unconsciously, comparison can cause you to rush. Trying to keep up with others in your industry and even your circle will set you up to be out of God's time. Observing other businesses should only encourage you to work harder but never push you outside of God's timing. If an unhealthy feeling of anxiety or pressure comes, take a step back and seek God for clarity. You should be at peace with wherever the Lord has you on his timeline. The mistakes of others could very well lead to success for you and vice versa. Just because a certain technique or approach to business works for someone else doesn't mean you will have the same success. It could actually set you back a few years or even financially. Comparing your progress to the word God has spoken concerning you should be the only thing to balance your successes with.

Comparison lined up with God's timing, is a proactive way to use comparison. However, there are a few reasons why comparison shouldn't be used by itself or without God's guidance. Imposter syndrome will have you feeling unqualified for the very thing God called you to do. Impostor syndrome is a mental flaw where someone constantly doubts their abilities and feels undeserving of their success, despite clear evidence of their skill and achievements, and the feeling of not being good enough. It can also lead to not submitting to God's will or lack of desire to accomplish what He has for you. This discouragement can be caused by feeling behind, not knowing the real journey of those who appear to be successful. The most alarming effect that comes from comparison without

The Comparison

confidence in yourself is loss of identity. Consciously or unconsciously trying to imitate other brands is very dangerous. Picking up someone else's mantle when God has another prepared just for you literally demonstrates your lack of trust in him. It also means you are trying to control the journey instead of letting Him lead. Lack of submission to the identity He placed in you and the unique story shared through your business will weaken your brand and affect its lifespan. Remember your journey for a successful brand should be merely guided by God.

THE MIND

Having the mind of Christ not only stabilizes your mind but also gives you the authority to create. Success in business is found by not only thinking like Christ but also creating like Christ. Using this fundamental understanding sets you apart from other industries built on worldly principles. As a child of God, we have the upper hand and insight on tactics to ascend and occupy the different mountains of influence: Religion, Family, Education, Government, Media, Arts & Entertainment, and Business.

Access to Christ 's mind is obtained by the building of a relationship with Him. This is done by daily intimate time with him through prayer, studying His word, and being in constant conversation with Holy Spirit. You have to know Him in order to hear His instructions and follow them. Without intentionally spending time with Him , you would have no idea when He is telling you to shift, build or even pause. Ignoring the ability to have access to the blueprint of success is self sabotage. As His children, by coming into agreement with His will, we welcome the grace to build.

The Mind

Renewing your mind to reflect His mind also keeps you relevant. He knows how to keep you in sync with His timing while being a vessel in the earth. We are demonstrators of His Will being done on earth as it is in heaven. We should be aware of where our thoughts are coming from. Keeping our personal opinion off of what God wants clears the path to letting His mind and thoughts lead your branding and building journey.

Having His mind is like having a security system wrapped around your brand. There's nothing that can infiltrate your business to hinder its growth if it is Christ-led from inception. The only thing that will slow its growth would be God Himself, but even that delay can be used to your favor. By working through a challenge or pivot one can realign and set the brand back on a progressive journey.

It's imperative to have the mind of Christ prior to launching. If you are already in your building process, it is perfectly fine to take a moment to self check. Assess where you are mentally. Mental stability is necessary. The journey at times can be a challenge, but only those with thoughts set on things above are guaranteed the grace to maneuver through being a brand owner.

Having a Christ-like mind is created by renewing your mind. It requires you to literally release your agenda and take on His thoughts for you. You should also be an earthly example of His desire to serve and love others. This is exhibited by not only walking in love but also in forgiveness. Having a hardened heart and lack of forgiveness is definitely a roadblock for some builders. You will not be able to freely build and grow with the weight and burden of unforgiveness on your shoulders. It also cuts you off from resources and the community that could supply things for you. The very person who has the key necessary for reaching the next season of

The Mind

potential for your business could very well be the person you refuse to forgive. Just because you think someone is not connected to your industry should not lead you to assume that they do not have access to things necessary for you to flourish in it. Striving for obedience and not success will also keep you in alignment with Christ's mind. You have to allow Holy Spirit to guide your thoughts and respond to His directions with swift obedience. By practicing these principles, you can develop a Christ-like mindset and create according to His will.

THE PROBLEM

Have you ever found yourself constantly irritated by different elements associated with a particular mountain of influence? I mean like burdened, and it really puts a weight on you when you experience it. If so, that is most likely the problem you are called to solve. The Lord puts irritants in the earth to get our attention. He is so amazing at how He created the earth and placed us here. He has you going through life, experiencing hardships, overcoming challenges, building your character, cultivating skills and wisdom, all while calling you to a mountain to use those same tools you have been graced with to confront a problem. Isn't He wonderful? I am always amazed at how God moves in multiple areas at one time.

The Mountains of Influence (Religion, Family, Education, Government, Media, Arts & Entertainment, and Business) are seven spheres that help shape society. As believers, our goal should be ascending these mountains, having influence on them, and letting our light draw mankind to God's kingdom. The problem is these

The Problem

mountains have been contaminated, perverted, and just down right made a mess of. All of the world belongs to God. We should be able to go in and overturn everything the enemy has tried to claim. As a vessel, we are created to see the problems and solve them. Everything you have gone through in life will prepare you to face the issues head on.

You will know which problem you are called to by how heavily it weighs on you. Are you burdened by the lack of financial literacy in your community? I guarantee you have probably experienced financial hardship at some point in your life, figured out a way to get yourself out of the poverty pit, that experience became wisdom, led you to research and get more skill, and now you have the ability to train others on how to do the same thing. That is the result of all things working together and reveals your testimony.

One successfully influences their Mountain of Influence by being set apart, being the light, going in exposing and transforming dark places. You can not go in and become the very thing you originally were trying to influence. Lack of relationship with Christ and not being His reflection in these spaces will lead you to a dead end road. Approaching the problem with Holiness is not about being churchy or beating someone over the head with the name of Jesus. It is about constantly demonstrating God's character and your actions, pointing all focus back to Him. While building brands that solve problems, God will uplift those who promote His agenda.

While ascending your mountain of influence, you need to have the skill and practical knowledge to maneuver through it. For instance, trying to ascend the mountain of Arts and Entertainment without any investment in a professional level experience (like a production on Broadway or even simply taking a class with technical training)

The Problem

will not get you very far. We have to partner our God-given gifts and abilities with training to perfect them. We should be able to keep up with those ascending the mountain with us. Holy Spirit will definitely lead you up, however you cannot just sit like a bump on a log and not hold your own weight. Knowing the craft or tools of your mountain will encourage those you are trying to influence to draw to God and to take you seriously. Not having a practical understanding of your mountain will not turn the ear of those who may be on the other side. Newly birthed businesses that are supposed to influence any mountain have to mirror Christ's traits and light. Building with a lack of skill and wisdom is a major problem. You can solve a problem while being one. Before releasing your brand, be sure to: fully understand the problem you are called to confront, take a deep dive into your life experiences, let your testimony lead you to the skills needed to overcome and influence, and let your set-apart life shine light on the problem as you govern your mountain.

THE SOLUTION

You are a God-sent solution to this earth. Take joy in the fact that God has equipped you with a testimony to build a brand, a business, a product, a ministry, a service that reflects His glory on the earth. Being and creating a solution will always lead you to success. It will enable you to serve people, communities, and their needs. One of the first questions you should ask yourself is how your business or product will play a role in being a solution. If you cannot answer that question, I suggest going back to the drawing board, better known as God's feet. Seeking Him will help expose the areas of your life where solutions were first planted and grown.

Come into agreement with God's will for your life. Delay is caused by not facing the reality of what is placed in us. Choosing God's way should disconnect us from selectively choosing the problems we want to produce solutions for. You can try, but it will not have a long lifespan. Solve what God directed you to, stay in your lane, and prosper. Trying to create outside of His will not only delay you,

The Solution

but it will also cause you to be in the way of other builders. So now not only are you out of alignment, but you are causing blockages for others. Grace and favor will chase you down when you are obedient to God and follow His path to sharing your solution.

Following heaven's blueprint for my life has led me through doors that I would have never touched in my own power. Striving for excellence in how I shared solutions has given me an indescribable peace with the decisions made, knowing that they have all brought God glory. It has prepared me with an ability to provide solutions that are effective and valuable. This is where you will be able to represent God in an honorable way.

How would one prepare to be the solution beyond cultivating their gifts and being vulnerable with their story? Intercession. As a solution, you are standing in the gap to deliver answers. Yes, your brand can be used as an intercessory tool. Your business should encourage others by providing services or products that give them confidence in multiple areas. It is servanthood, just like Christ, our Intercessor.

Your solution should demonstrate and be according to the grace given to you. It is a measure that God gives to us and we should stay under that umbrella. Going outside of that becomes dangerous since you would now be operating in your own strength. God is not obligated to provide favor and resource when you have ventured outside of His purpose and calling for you. Building with the grace He provides will yield fruit. Committing to God before you start will release everything you need for your business plans. Being in His will with tools and guidance that were downloaded from seeking Him, with solutions that were highlighted and cultivated from life challenges, and the ability to use your story to send focus back to

The Solution

what God has done will give you the confidence to launch your brand with and in purpose.

THE PRAYER

Father, in the name of Jesus,

You are amazing. You are wonderful. You are awesome in all of Your ways. There is no one like You, and I give You all the glory. You are worthy of all the praise; You are worthy of all the honor.

I thank You. I thank You for being my provider and showing yourself as Jireh. I thank You for being all that I need. Without You, I am nothing.

I am grateful for every word You have released through me. I am grateful for everything You have done. For every resource You have provided, for the favor and grace that follows me, I thank You.

Lord, I ask You to make us pure vessels. Vessels to be used on this earth, pure vessels to carry Your glory, pure vessels to walk out the purpose You have called us to. I ask You to forgive us of our sins,

The Prayer

both known and unknown. God, make us pure builders, set apart. Let us reflect on Your light in all areas of our lives. Let us be image bearers in the Mountains of Influence and in every industry.

Father, I lift up these builders to You. The creators and those whom You have called. I ask You to bless them. Bless their hands so that whatever they touch shall prosper. Bless their minds so that all their thoughts are clear. Bless their feet so that every room they walk into causes every imp there to flee.

Father, in the name of Jesus, I ask You to bless the doors and opportunities that come their way. Let them understand and have clear discernment to recognize what You have sent. Strengthen their discernment, Lord God, so they can distinguish the business connections they need to pour into and those they should disconnect from. Bless the circles they enter that you have directed them to. In the name of Jesus, I pray that every space they enter into will be governed by the Holy Spirit.

God, I ask You to give them strength and confidence to build the things You have called them to. Soften their hearts so they may be vulnerable enough to share the stories You have given them.

In the name of Jesus, let Your will be done in their lives and not only bring them into alignment, but also agreement with it. For every resource, every financial need, and every idea, I ask You to release it to those who seek your face and are called to build. Let them unlock their divine purpose by seeking Your face. Let the name of Jesus be lifted up as the result of their obedience, and let it yield fruit. You get all the glory.

The Prayer

I declare that this book will realign every agenda, every desire, every walk, every thought, every decision with God's purpose and character.

In Jesus' name, Amen.

LIVE YOUR DREAMS CHALLENGE

Welcome to the 7 day *Live Your Dreams Challenge*. Follow along to awaken your gifts and begin the journey of bringing your dreams to life.

Live Your Dreams Challenge

DAY 1

Explore the endless possibilities. What if the thought or fear of failure wasn't an option?

Where does your mind naturally wander when you daydream? Now, what if I told you that whatever you're dreaming can become your reality, your life? Does the thought of that scare you? Do you find yourself pulling back, putting limits on your imagination? Don't run from it! Embrace it. What goals would you attempt to conquer if failure wasn't an option? Take a moment today to let your thoughts flow freely as you prepare to create goals and future achievements. Write them down as the thoughts come and you might surprise yourself. Enjoy your explorations!

_____

_____

_____

_____

_____

_____

DAY 2

What issues would your achievements and goals solve?

Now that you have explored the possibilities of what your goals could be, let's focus on how they can be beneficial.

Success for an individual, comes from creating or being the answer to an issue. For example, I am a full time freelance makeup artist. I am available during the day to work with photographers. The Issue: Many photographers struggle to find makeup artists with availability during typical shoot times, as most artists work full-time jobs and have limited flexibility. The Solution: As a makeup artist with a flexible schedule, I'm available during the times photographers need most. This makes it easier for them to book shoots, meet client demands, and ultimately boost revenue for everyone involved.

Today, review the goals you've created; figure out how they will solve some of the issues of the world we live in and simultaneously bring you success.

_____

_____

_____

Live Your Dreams Challenge

DAY 3

Evaluate your passions and define your purpose?

We often follow our passion, but there's one small issue with that. Passion is connected to our emotions. And because our emotions are not always consistent, it's not beneficial to base our goals or careers on passion alone. Purpose should be the true driving force behind what we do. We were all created for a reason. The hard part is identifying it. Passion often feels gratifying while purpose serves the needs of others.

Take some time today for introspection. Identify both your passion and purpose. Compare and contrast the two to determine how your purpose connects with yesterday's reflection: how your goals and achievements can help solve issues in the world around you.

_____

_____

_____

_____

_____

Live Your Dreams Challenge

DAY 4

Determine the requirements needed to reach your ultimate goal and break them down into smaller achievable goals.

Now we are almost ready to put all of our preparation into action. Sometimes, goals can seem unreachable and overwhelming. The best way to eliminate that feeling is simply by breaking your final goal into manageable steps. Background research will be essential for this phase as there may be prerequisites to attain certain goals. For example, if your goal is to become a doctor, you would be required to complete medical school and pass specific exams. You can't just walk into any hospital with your little goal book and say "Hi, I'm here to be a doctor!" There's a necessary process between setting goals and making them a reality.

Once you've completed your background research, document each step necessary to accomplish your goal and assign target dates for each. Target dates keep you focused and accountable. Be sure your documentation is as detailed as possible, list everything from applying for scholarships, creating a website, taking professional headshots, and so on. Using this method will definitely make the journey towards your goal more enjoyable.

Live Your Dreams Challenge

DAY 5

Identify idle moments in your day that should be replaced with time spent working towards your end goal.

I always cringe at the excuse: "I don't have time." I've grown to believe that people make time for what they want. Be very careful about using time as an excuse for not working towards your goals. Instead of scrolling on social media, napping or binge watching your favorite Netflix shows, use that time to research and check off items on your goal list. Make the decision to intentionally break that habit. Choose to not waste time on things that aren't beneficial to your personal growth or for building your brand. Hold yourself accountable, and before you know it, you'll have a new set of healthy habits.

_____
_____
_____
_____
_____
_____
_____

Live Your Dreams Challenge

DAY 6

How much faith do you have in the gifts God gave you?

On this journey to reaching your goals, there may be moments when you lack motivation. The question above always makes me refocus and puts some fire back in me.

James 2:17 says, "Thus also faith by itself, if it does not have works, is dead." As we check off our goal lists, we are showing how faith is an action word. Our faith in God should motivate us to work toward the gifts He gave us. No work, No faith. No faith, no work.

Live Your Dreams Challenge

DAY 7

"Delight yourself also in the Lord, And He shall give you the desires of your heart." - Psalm 37:4 KJV

As the *Live Your Dreams Challenge* comes to an end, it is my prayer that you have stepped outside of your box and pushed beyond your comfort zone. I hope that my personal strategies shared have opened your eyes to a new way of approaching the process of achieving goals. It may be the last day of this particular challenge, but I encourage you to continue pushing toward your desires.

The most important part of this overall process is to keep God first. Everything falls into place when you pursue Him before any worldly goal. Your main focus and priority should be worshiping Him ("But seek first..." Matthew 6:33). Give Him his honor and then organize everything else. There is a unique balancing act that occurs when mastering the goal process that gives God all the glory the entire time. Meditate on Psalms 37:4 today, and evaluate the order of your priorities.

_____

_____

_____

_____

ABOUT THE AUTHOR

Jeanna Booker is a creative entrepreneur dedicated to cultivating creativity, purpose, and excellence in others. She is a proud graduate of the Baltimore School for the Arts, where she majored in Visual Arts, and later attended the Maryland Institute College of Art, majoring in photography. Jeanna has built a dynamic career that bridges artistry, faith, and empowerment.

In 2012, she founded 13:46 Dance Ensemble, a Christian-based company that has since grown to include multiple ensembles across the U.S. and internationally. Under her leadership, the company has ministered at numerous events, including live recordings for gospel artists like Maranda Curtis and Psalmist Raine, fusing choreography with worship to transform atmospheres and demonstrate Gods heart.

Jeanna has led and choreographed for several dance ministries, mentored upcoming movement leaders, and traveled nationally and abroad to facilitate conferences, workshops, and creative intensives. She is known for using movements that convey testimonies as a tool to teach, inspire, and activate purpose.

Beyond dance, Jeanna is a skilled visual artist, certified makeup artist with a passion for mortuary makeup, creative director, and graphic designer. Her work spans industries, from doing makeup for Alvin Ailey's tour promotions and multiple celebrity clients, to directing photoshoots and branding experiences for entrepreneurs and artists. As a full-time entrepreneur, she uses her business and artistic expertise to guide others in launching and elevating their own visions.

Jeanna is a visionary with a heart for creatives and a divine ability to awaken dormant gifts in others. Every adversity she's faced has been turned into a platform to glorify God. Whether on stage, behind the scenes, or in one-on-one mentorship, her mission remains clear: to spark innovation, awaken purpose, and empower others to boldly step into their God-given calling.

BOOKING & INQUIRIES

I'm currently accepting bookings for panels, creative classes, and one-on-one sessions. Whether you're looking for insight on entrepreneurship, choreography, makeup artistry, or dance technique, I'd love to be part of your next event or project. From workshops and conferences to intimate coaching sessions, I bring a passion for artistry and empowerment to every space I step into. Let's create something unforgettable together.

To book or connect with me, please email JeannaBCreative@gmail.com or visit www.JeannaBCreative.com.

LETS CONNECT

Follow and subscribe to stay in the loop with all the amazing things happening with Jeanna B.

Jeanna B.
Instagram: @JeannaBooker
Facebook: Jeanna Booker
JeannaBCreative@gmail.com
www.JeannaBCreative.com

Dance
Instagram: @1346DanceEnsemble
Facebook: 13 46 Dance Ensemble
13.46Dance@gmail.com
www.1346Dance.com

MakeUp
Instagram: @Mua_JeannaB
Mua.JeannaB@gmail.com
www.JeannaBCreative.com

Art and Graphics
Instagram: @JeannaBCreative
JeannaBCreative@gmail.com
www.JeannaBCreative.com

Not sure what to do next and have questions about entrepreneurship, branding, or just need a second opinion about your business? Book your "Office Hours" at JeannaBCreative.com.

MEDIA RESOURCES

To further support you on your journey, here are some resources I've personally found helpful and encourage you to explore:

Instagram:
@akosua_asa
@dontellantonio
@mahdiwoodard
@socialdox

Tools and Apps:
Canva
PowerDirctor

Photographer:
Derek Chase
@thephotochase
www.thephotochase.com

Devotionals from the Bible App:
Why Art Matters for the Christian
The Mountains Are Calling
H3 Leadership
Heart of Worship
The Pursuit
Unraveling The Scriptures For Leadership Effectiveness

www.ingramcontent.com/pod-product-compliance
Lightning Source LLC
Chambersburg PA
CBHW071122160426
43196CB00013B/2669